AWESOME AGRICULTURE

CORN

an A-to-Z book

Susan Anderson & JoAnne Buggey

Book design by Nancy Roberts

Northwest Arm Press

This book is dedicated to Bob

Tractor illustrations by Gerry Cleary,
from an original idea by James Jahoda

Northwest Arm Press, Inc.
1004-1545 South Park Street
Halifax Nova Scotia Canada B3J 4B3

Project photographer: Lisa Marie Noseworthy, LMNO Photo
Fact-checking: Paddy Muir

Special thanks to Mark Hamerlinck,
Minnesota Corn Growers Association

Models:
B: Sarah Howlett
G: left, Jean Hoff
L: Sebastien Bien-Aimé
O: l. to r., Gail Moran, Grace Moran
P: l. to r., Hugh Fox, Jazla Cook, Sagar Kumar

This product conforms to CPSIA 2011.
Printed in China

Library and Archives Canada Cataloguing in Publication

Anderson, Susan, 1950-
    Awesome agriculture : corn : an A-to-Z book / Susan Anderson, JoAnne
Buggey.

(Awesome agriculture for kids)
ISBN 978-1-926781-02-0

    1. Corn--Juvenile literature. 2. English language--Alphabet--Juvenile
literature. 3. Alphabet books. I. Buggey, JoAnne II. Title. III. Series:
Awesome agriculture for kids

SB191.M2A55 2011   j633.1'5   C2011-900356-2

Hello!

I'm Agri-Culture. Call me Agri.

You will see me on every page of this book about corn.

Each page contains

- A letter of the alphabet
- A word about corn beginning with that letter
- A picture and information to help you understand the word
- ME to help you learn more about each word

Let's start with **Aa** on the next page...

Aa

This is a field of corn. Farmers who grow corn are corn producers.

agriculture

Agriculture is awesome. Corn is a part of agriculture.

Bb

Corn is measured by the bushel.

bushel

This is a bushel of corn.

Cc

ears

stalks

There are usually one or two good ears of corn on each stalk.

corn

Corn grows on stalks like these.

Dd

This is called "dent corn" because the kernels have dents in them. Dent corn is also called field corn.

dent

There are different kinds of corn. Dent corn is the kind of corn grown on most farms.

Ee

Refineries like this one turn corn into ethanol, a fuel that can be mixed with gasoline to power cars.

energy

Corn is a source of renewable energy.

Ff

feed

Almost half the field corn grown in the United States is used to feed animals.

Gg

Look in your grocery store to see if you can find foods that are made with corn.

grocery store

Corn is found in many products throughout your grocery store.

Hh

A combine is one machine that can be used to harvest corn.

harvest

It is fall. This field of corn is ready to harvest.

Ii

This is one way to irrigate.

irrigation

In areas where there is not enough rainfall, corn producers might use irrigation to provide the needed water.

Jj

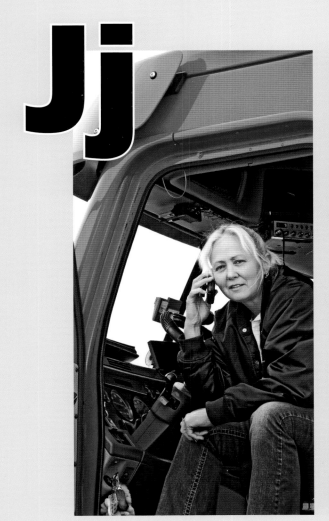

These people do not work on farms.

jobs

Many people have jobs to help corn producers.

Kk

This is the size of a kernel of corn.

kernels

All ears of corn are covered with kernels.
The kernels are attached to the cob.

Ll

How do you like to eat corn?

like

Another kind of corn is sweet corn. Most people like to eat sweet corn.

SCP2-b

Mm

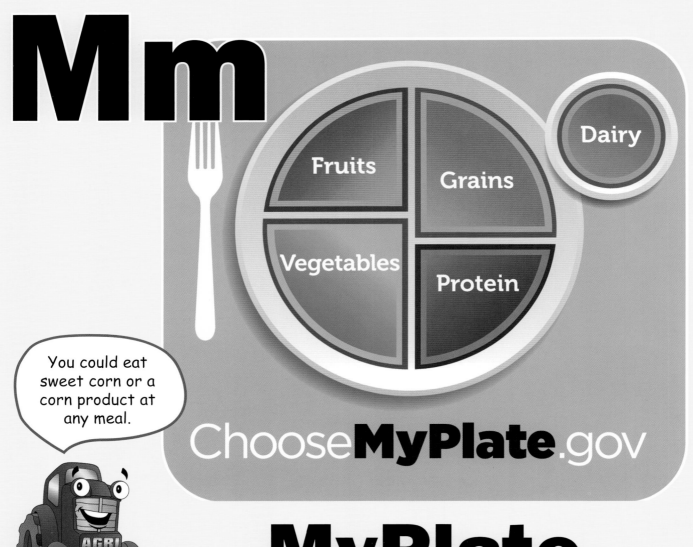

MyPlate

Corn is in either the Vegetables or the Grains section
of MyPlate depending on how it is prepared.

Nn

nutrition

Eating corn is important for good nutrition.

Which of these corn products have you tried?

Oo

Ask how corn oil is used where you live.

oil

Many people cook with corn oil.

Pp

When you heat kernels of popcorn, they pop. That is why it is called popcorn.

popcorn

Popcorn is another kind of corn people like to eat.
It can be a healthy snack.

Qq

This farm is being used to test different kinds of corn.

quality

Corn growers want the best quality corn.

Rr

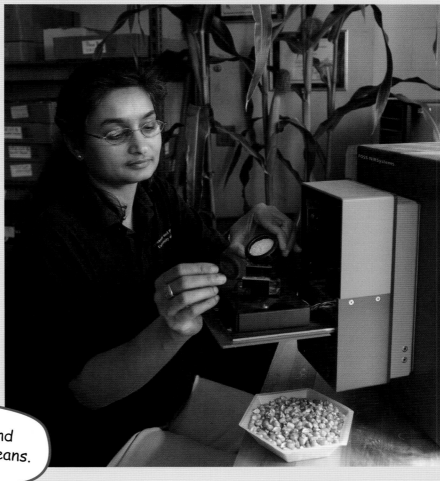

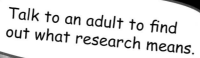
Talk to an adult to find out what research means.

research

Research is being done around the world to find new uses for corn.

Ss

tassels

silks

Pollen falls from the tassels onto the silks.

silks

Silks are an important part of each ear of corn. A kernel must be attached to a silk in order to grow.

Tt

Corn might be moved by tractors, trucks, trains, barges, and ships.

transportation

Many kinds of transportation are used to deliver corn from the farm to other places.

Uu

The top corn-producing states are Illinois, Indiana, Iowa, Minnesota, and Nebraska.

United States

Corn is grown throughout the United States. The states in color grow most of the corn.

Vv

Corn producers are growing more than enough corn to make all of these products.

versatile

Corn is a versatile crop. It's used for many things beyond food and fuel.

Ww

Good weather is necessary for planting, growing, and harvesting corn.

weather

Weather conditions such as sunshine and rain are important for producing good corn.

Xx

INGREDIENTS: WATER, BEEF, TOMATOES, PINK BEANS, KIDNEY BEANS, TOMATO PASTE, DEHYDRATED ONIONS, CHILI SEASONING (SPICES, SUGAR, SALT, FLAVOUR), MODIFIED CORNSTARCH, JALAPENO PEPPERS (VINEGAR, FLAVOUR, SALT, DEHYDRATED BELL PEPPERS, SPICES.

Look for corn on the labels of food products you eat.

AGRI

x marks the spot

Find X on the label. It shows that corn is in this product.

Yy

you

What did you learn about corn?

Zz

Z to A or A to Z

Corn is awesome! We all agree.

activities

to do with an adult

Make a corn snack.

You will need
- 1 cup each of 5 cereals containing corn
- 1 cup of peanuts, raisins, or M&Ms (optional)
- 12 plastic sandwich bags

Mix the ingredients in a large bowl. Divide the mixture into 12 servings (about 1/2 cup each). Put one serving in each bag.

Other activities:

- Try some of the activities that Agri suggests in the book.

- When you are riding in the car, look for a field of corn.

- Make a list of all the ways you have eaten corn.

- Look at your cereal boxes. How many of the cereals include corn?

- Collect labels that include corn products.

- Make up a song or poem about corn.

More titles in the
Awesome Agriculture A-to-Z series

Soybeans, an A-to-Z book, 2009
*American Farm Bureau Federation
2010 PreK-K Accurate Ag Book*

Pigs, an A-to-Z book, 2010

Corn, an A-to-Z book, 2011

forthcoming...
    Beef
    Wheat
    Dairy
    Poultry

For children 8–11,
The Story of Agriculture series

Soybeans in the Story of Agriculture
*American Farm Bureau Federation
2010 Book of the Year*

Pigs & Pork in the Story of Agriculture, 2010

forthcoming...
    Corn
    Beef
    Wheat
    Dairy
    Poultry

Both soybean books are also Illinois Ag in the Classroom 2010 Ag Week Books of the Year. *Soybeans in the Story of Agriculture* is also Minnesota Farm Bureau 2010 Book of the Year.

The Authors

JoAnne Buggey has a PhD in Curriculum & Instruction from the University of Washington (1971). She taught future elementary teachers in the College of Education and Human Development at the University of Minnesota. JoAnne has written dozens of textbooks for children including an American history text, *America! America!* and a civics text, *Civics for Americans.* Her recent multimedia projects include Exploring Where and Why, a program on maps and mapping for grades K–3.

Susan Anderson earned her MS in Curriculum & Instruction from Minnesota State University, Mankato (1988). She is an Education Specialist for University of Minnesota Extension in the College of Food, Agricultural and Natural Resource Sciences. Susan grew up on a farm and lives on a working farm today. During her elementary teaching years she developed an interdisciplinary fifth-grade curriculum to increase agricultural literacy.

Both authors have been elementary teachers in the Minneapolis Public Schools. They currently work with the K-12 Education Program at the University of Minnesota Southwest Research and Outreach Center at Lamberton. They provide workshops for future and current elementary teachers in agricultural literacy. Both have contributed to curriculum projects including materials related to dairy and pigs. The authors serve on various boards related to agriculture and have won awards for quality teaching about agriculture. JoAnne and Susan are currently part of an Improving Teacher Quality grant team.

Acknowledgements

For invaluable assistance, our thanks to David Hansen, University of Minnesota; Curtis MacPhee; Katherine Howlett; Ned Fox; and Wendy Mills.

Image Credits